HELP FOR MORAL INJURY: STRATEGIES AND INTERVENTIONS

Cecilia Yocum, PhD

Forward by Lynn Newsom

Quaker House

HELP FOR MORAL INJURY:
STRATEGIES AND INTERVENTIONS

Copyright © 2016

Published by:

Quaker House of Fayetteville, NC

223 Hillside Ave.

Fayetteville, North Carolina, 28301

www.quakerhouse.org

910-323-3912

Photos and Cover Art Design by: Leslie Lingo

ISBN-13: 978-1533064882

ISBN-10: 1533064881

Quaker House is a manifestation of the Religious Society of Friends' Peace Testimony. Based in Fayetteville, North Carolina, the home of Fort Bragg, Quaker House provides counseling and support for service members, veterans, their families, and the public about military issues; and advocates for a more peaceful world.

The GI Rights Hotline offers free, accurate, non-directive information about issues of conscience, discharge, medical, psychological, and other regulations: 877-477-4487

Military and Veterans' Domestic Violence, Sexual Assault, and Moral Injury Counseling Hotline: 904-274-3571

TABLE OF CONTENTS

Reproduction of Contents

Help for Moral Injury: Strategies and Interventions

Cecilia Yocum, Ph.D.

Foreword by Lynn Newsom

Quaker House is a manifestation of the Religious Society of Friends' Peace Testimony. Based in Fayetteville, North Carolina, home of Fort Bragg, Quaker House provides counseling and support to service members who are questioning their role in the military; educates them, their families, and the public about military issues; and advocates for a more peaceful world.

Steve and Lynn Newsom have been the co-directors of Quaker House since December 2012. Both are longtime members of the Religious Society of Friends and served on the Board of Quaker House before becoming co-directors. Since they have been at Quaker House, they have worked to educate the public on the issues involved in the use of militarized drones and torture, connected with military and community mental health care providers to provide free counseling for military domestic violence, sexual assault, and moral injury victims, continued counseling for service members on their rights, conducted Alternatives to Violence Project (AVP) training, and worked to create a positive public peace witness in the community through newspaper interviews, public appearances and house concerts.

At the invitation of a coalition of faith communities in Raleigh, North Carolina, Quaker House co-sponsored a conference in March 2014, titled "Soul Repair Journey: Recovering from Moral Injury after War." This conference, led by Rev. Rita Nakashima Brock, co-founder of the Brite Divinity School Soul Repair Center, Texas, inspired Lynn and Steve to begin providing education on "moral injury." They realized that since the founding of Quaker House in 1969, many of the service members and veterans came, and still come, asking for help with moral injury issues.

The relatively new diagnosis of moral injury, accepted by the VA, challenges Quaker House to step into a stronger role in counseling service members. We believe that it is more important than ever that faith communities seek to understand that our service members are suffering in increasing numbers from the wounds to the conscience brought on by continued wars and we must be prepared to help them. Consequently, Quaker House has expanded its therapy to include moral injury victims and works hard to reach out to the military, veteran, and civilian communities to help them understand what moral injury is and what we can do to help and support those who suffer from it.

Dr. Cecilia Yocum has put together a booklet of strategies and interventions that could be used to help people cope with moral injury issues. We are so thankful to her for her generosity and compassion.

About Dr. Yocum

Cecilia Yocum received her Ph.D. in psychology from Ohio State University in 1978. She has over 35 years of experience working with individuals, families, communities, and professional groups. Dr. Yocum has also worked overseas with community-based trauma healing programs in Rwanda, Burundi, and Colombia as a part of Friends Peace Teams.

Dr. Yocum has been actively involved with Alternatives to Violence Project workshops at Coleman Federal Correctional Institution for many years, as a facilitator through the Tampa Bay AVP Council. She is a past board member of the Florida Center for Survivors of Torture, and has provided psychological evaluations for political asylum seekers. In 2006, she received the "Outstanding Contributions to Psychology in the Public Interest" award from the Florida Psychological Association.

A brief discussion of what is meant by moral injury

(Contributed by Beverly Ward Ph.D., with additions by Dr. Yocum)

Events do not occur in a vacuum. If an act of violence occurs both the wounded and the agent suffer. In the United States we have been late to recognize and provide supportive services to victims of post-traumatic stress disorder, and are only beginning to recognize a need to address moral injury – debilitating guilt, shame and self-condemnation secondary to inflicting violence State-sanctioned or otherwise, on others. Both exist. Both haunt our society.

Dr. Rita Nakashima Brock uses the concept of feeling spiritually lost or broken, or being heartbroken, to describe the effects of moral injury. It will be important to find out what terms or languages are used by the people you work with, and how they prefer to describe their condition.

The strategies and interventions provided in this booklet set forth a means of addressing the injuries to an individual's moral codes. The conflict or tension with one's personal codes and that of armed conflict and the aftermath may create conditions which can make it difficult to return to "normal" life. The strategies and interventions provided here are opportunities for individuals to identify, address, and manage those conflicts or tensions through a structured process and, above all, in a safe supportive environment.

Practitioners are encouraged to assess the strategies and interventions described in this booklet and to incorporate them into their therapeutic strategies as appropriate. The emphasis is on recognizing that agents of injury also suffer, identifying the nature of their emotional and spiritual injuries, and providing a safe environment to facilitate healing.

Background for these exercises

In **Moral Injury** by Alice Lynd and Staughton Lynd, the author cited the work of Nash, Westphal and Litz, (see references and resources below) presented at an Armed Forces Health Conference (3/23/11). Methods and goals of treatment for moral injury were listed as:

- Rationally seeking to assess one's own or others' culpability

- Making or seeking amends

- Compassionate forgiveness of self and others

This set of activities will help those with moral injury develop some tools to work toward the goals listed above along with other goals of understanding moral injury, self-care, and developing personal and spiritual resources. These exercises/activities are designed to be used by counselors/pastoral counselors, psychologists or other mental health workers.

Some of the exercises use methods that are grounded in Gestalt, psychodrama, Alternatives to Violence, Cognitive Therapy, and other methods. It is strongly recommended that those who are not familiar with this type of work should seek consultation from experienced practitioners.

3

These exercises are based on the work of Friends Peace Teams in Burundi, Rwanda, El Salvador, Guatemala, Honduras, and Colombia. Also, some activities are adapted from Alternatives to Violence work with prisoners, who often have moral injury issues. In addition, some of the psychodrama activities have been used in therapy with people who have moral injury issues.

These exercises are not intended for people with substance abuse issues, suicidal thinking or thoughts of hurting others or severe mental illness, or with severe anger issues.

DISCLAIMER:

The activities and exercises provided below have not been evaluated through evidence-based research with veterans. This publication is offered in the hope that the methods presented will be useful in conjunction with other therapies provided by the Veterans Administration and similar counseling groups. Trauma healing activities in the U.S. and overseas have found these techniques useful in working with civilian and ex-combatant victims of moral injury in the aftermath of wars and political atrocities.

LANGUAGE:

This booklet recognizes that moral injury knows no boundaries: military, veteran, civilian, male, female, adult, or youth. Rather than using only plural pronouns throughout this booklet, this publication has specifically chosen to mix the third person singular with the third person plural, for example: Ask the person what led them to seek help. This booklet will also use veteran and person interchangeably.

ACKNOWLEDGEMENTS:

This collection would not be possible without the help of numerous people including Lynn Newsom, Nina Garcia, Christina Bellamy, Linda Condon, and others. Thanks to Dr. Beverly Ward and Steve Kinney for editing and other suggestions.

SECTION ONE: INTRODUCTION FOR COUNSELORS

1.1 - Preparing to work with people with moral injury:

1. Consult the resources listed in the Section 9 below for background and details on the subject of moral injury. New information is coming out all the time.

2. Seek out a supervisor or peer with whom you can consult. You will probably hear some very intense and difficult stories. It is important to take good care of yourself. Debrief with someone else, if needed, so you do not internalize the stress from the stories.

3. Some of these exercises use action methods that are grounded in Gestalt, psychodrama, and other experiential therapies. It is strongly recommended that those who are not experienced in this kind of work seek consultation from therapists who can assist them. The author may be available for consultation and can be contacted at ceceyocum@aol.com.

1.2 – Intake interview

You would perform your usual intake and discuss confidentiality issues. Screen for substance abuse issues, suicide or thoughts of hurting others, severe mental illness, or severe anger issues. If these issues are present, they would need to be addressed and treated first either by you or another counselor.

Assuming you believe that this person has issues related to moral injury, you should then discuss the concept of moral injury.

Some people will be ready to jump right in and start talking about what is bothering them. You might then weave in some of the resources as you go along.

1.3 - Helping people to understand moral injury:

1. Ask the person what led them to seek help, and what they already know about moral injury. What reading have they done on the subject? What have they heard about moral injury? How do they see themselves in relation to moral injury?

2. Resources listed in the Section 10 may help people learn more about moral injury. Some people will have read a lot and some will have not read anything.

3. Ask if they have looked into other resources, i.e. veterans' organizations, pastoral care, community organizations, veterans' support groups, etc.

4. Ask if they have checked into the resources at the VA. Explain that their local VA might have programs such as the Impact of Killing and Adaptive Disclosure programs available. Provide contact information for local support resources relevant to moral injury if they are interested.

5. Provide psycho-educational information from the slides from Quaker House about the difference between PTSD and moral injury. Give the person a copy of the chart "Symptoms of moral injury v. PTSD." [Section 11, MORAL INJURY POWERPOINT page 4.] Do they see their concerns on this chart and if so, where? Explain that there is a significant overlap between moral injury and PTSD but the focus of these exercises is moral injury. These exercises were not developed for PTSD, and someone would require different treatment for PTSD.

1.4 - Describe and explain some of the activities you could provide:

1. Tell them some of the subjects and types of activities you might be doing with them. Help them decide what would be most useful to them. It is recommended that they have some self-care and spiritual resources available to them as a base for the sessions.

2. Explain that one of the goals is to help use skills, tools, resources, and strengths they already have to help deal with problems arising from moral injury.

3. Let them know that these exercises have not been researched for moral injury at this time with veterans. They have been used for similar types of problems.

4. Explain that this is a collaborative approach and you might suggest some exercises but they can decline or choose some other exercises instead.

5. As the counselor you might have some ideas what exercises would be important for this person and you can explain why they might want to try them.

6. You do not need to do all of the exercises within each section and it will be up to your clinical judgment which exercise(s) will be best for each person. You should decide with the client which exercises are appropriate and what additional therapy you might provide from your own professional background.

7. Discuss their goals for this type of counseling and how they would know when they have achieved their goals.

8. Discuss if they have other concerns outside of moral injury and how or whether you might address them in the counseling or whether another counselor or resource would be more appropriate for those goals.

SECTION TWO: SUPPORT FOR HEALTHY LIFESTYLES

Purpose: Explain that having good self-care will help them when dealing with moral injury issues. Also, sometimes when people are feeling guilt or sorrow they feel unworthy of good self-care, when they actually need more self-care.

2.1 - Exercise: Stand on the line

Purpose: To assess self-care activities they have used in the past and present and would like to use in the future.

Instructions:

1. Brainstorm positive self-care activities. What are some of the things they have done or considered doing for self-care?

2. Ask the person to stand on an imaginary line from 1 to 100, according to the number that represents their previous level of self-care before entering the service. What were some of the things they found beneficial (not what they failed to do)? Make a list of these with them. If someone does not want to stand to do this exercise, you could draw the line on a sheet of paper.

3. Next ask the person to stand on an imaginary line from 1 to 100, according to the number that represents their current level of self-care. What are some of the activities they presently find beneficial? Did they start doing new things? Did they stop doing things they used to like to do? Make a list with them.

4. Next ask them to place themselves on the number where they would like be in the future. Ask what they could do to reach that number. Would there be anything they would have to give up to reach that number? What would they have to add? Make a list with them.

Reflect on the exercise with them. What did they learn? How did it feel to think about their self-care? What are some of the self-care techniques they would like to try on their own? Why is it important to seek self-care strategies when we are experiencing moral injury or loss?

You may ask them to imagine themselves participating in one or more of those activities. Ask them to describe the scene and its surroundings as vividly as possible; is anyone else there with them, and if so, who? Ask how they could carry out this activity in real life. Invite them to think of the steps they could follow to actually engage in the activity.

2.2 - Deep breathing

(Adapted from Peacebuilding en las Américas Trauma Resiliency workshop)

Purpose: To help the person learn to relax which will promote better thinking and problem solving. Below is one example; you might have some deep breathing exercises you like instead.

Instructions: Invite the participant to sit up straight in their chair, their feet firmly planted on the floor. Suggest that they close their eyes. Read or say these instructions slowly and calmly:

"Now breathe. Exhale. Inhale. Exhale.

Focus on your breath, which fills your lungs deeply.

Feel your breath as it comes out your nose. Inhale. Exhale. Inhale. Exhale.

If you feel your mind is scattered, return to concentrate on your breathing.

You're alive. You are here.

Imagine taking care of yourself with a healthy diet and exercise.

Allow yourself to let people you trust know your needs.

Take the opportunity to open up to other ways of healing whose source is outside of you and also inside of you.

Be willing to reach to the depths of your strength and inner resources.

As you exhale, let go of your pain, your disappointments, and your fatigue.

As you inhale, allow the air to bring reassuring calm to you. Inhale, exhale, inhale, exhale.

As you inhale, take in vital energy; fill yourself with well-being, experience peace."

Pause for a time allowing participants to relax their breathing.

Then, calmly say, *"Now you feel calm, relaxed, quietly prepare to open your eyes and return to this space. When you're ready, open your eyes, and look around."*

2.3 - Alternative relaxation exercises:

- If time is very short, take deep breaths in silence.

- Or take 3 - 5 breaths in silence.

- Drop Anchor: Ask the person to breathe and think of their breath dropping like an anchor deep within themselves and resting there for a little while.

- Develop your own words for a breathing exercise or ask the person to develop one for themselves and record these.

- Obtain a phone app for meditation. Many are available for free from Veterans Affairs such as PTSD Mindfulness Coach.

Reflections on relaxation techniques:

- *How do you feel using them?*

- *How can you use these activities in your daily life?*

- *What other ways can you can relax when you feel worried or anxious?*

2.4 - Exercise: self-care physical relaxation exercise

(Adapted from Peacebuilding en las Américas Trauma Resiliency workshop)

Purpose: To introduce a technique that can be used for relaxation and to calm oneself. Below is one example; you might have some deep breathing exercises you like instead.

Instructions: Invite the participant to sit up straight in their chair and put their feet firmly on the floor. Say, "If you feel pain in a part of your body, do not tense that part in the exercise. If you notice a pain beginning, please relax and stop exercising that part."

Suggest that the person close their eyes or focus on a fixed spot on the floor.

Explain slowly and calmly; when saying, "relax," let your breath out audibly:

"Breathe. Exhale. Inhale. Exhale. Focus on your breathing while you feel your lungs fill deeply. Notice your breath as you breathe out through your nose. Inhale. Exhale. Inhale. Exhale If you feel that your mind is wandering, focus gently back to your breathing. Inhale. Exhale. You're alive, you are here. As you inhale, take that vital energy, fill yourself with well-being, fill yourself with peace.

Now, start stretching your legs as straight and hard you can ... relax. Stretch your legs again. Move your foot up towards you, hold it like that ... move your feet down, out, hold and relax ...

Now tighten the muscles of your calves and your thighs. Squeeze, hold, and feel the tension in your legs. Exhale and relax. Return to your original position and let the muscles in your feet, your calves, and your thighs relax and be completely loose. Let your legs relax completely. And now feel this great relaxation from your toes to your calves and thighs. Feel very relaxed, or calm. Calm, relaxed.

Now suck in your stomach and make your whole abdomen hard. Hold it and feel the way your breath is cut off, feel the tightness in your belly. Exhale and let your belly relax; let your next breath fill it up.

Now stretch out your arms. Make two fists; tighten the muscles of your hands. Feel the tension, hold, hold, and relax. Let your arms return to their resting position. Feel the relaxation. Now extend your arms again. Tighten the muscles in your wrists, your lower arm, hold, hold and feel the tightness in your arms. Exhale and release them, release them and let your arms return to their original position. Stop for a second, take a moment, and notice the relaxation of your fingers, your hands, your upper arms, your lower arms. Let your arms be completely loose. Take a moment to experience the feeling of relaxation. Very relaxed and calm, very relaxed and calm.

Now arch your back backwards, raise your chest. Tighten the muscles in your chest, your abdomen, your back and neck. Hold it, hold it, and then let go of all tension. Let go of all tension. Note the relaxation of your muscles. Take a moment to feel the muscles relax in your chest, your abdomen, your neck, across your back. All your muscles will feel relaxed.

Now raise your shoulders up toward your ears, like you are shrugging. Hold them there and feel the tension. Now exhale, and let them sink back down in relaxation. Notice any tightness in your shoulders and arms and move them and breathe into the tension to relax those areas.

Now squeeze the muscles in your face, first the muscles of your forehead and then the muscles of the eyes. Tighten it. Hold it... hold it... exhale and relax. Now squeeze the muscles of your cheeks, the muscles of your mouth, the muscles of your chin. Tighten it. Hold it, hold it, and relax. Let all the muscles of the face relax, first the muscles of the chin, then the mouth, cheek muscles, muscles around the eyes, the muscles of the forehead. Release all tension from your face. Bite down hard with your teeth. Feel the tightness in your face, your jaw. Exhale and let your jaw and tongue relax. Let your chin drop, if you feel like it.

Take your time and enjoy the relaxation. You are very relaxed and calm, relaxed and calm.

Now, breathe through your nose slowly and deeply. Breathe into your throat first, your chest, then your abdomen. Hold your breath, hold it, and let it out slowly through your nose. Feel the relaxation. Inhale, holding, exhale, relax. Again inhale deeply, hold, hold, and slowly let it go. Release all the tension, your frustrations, your anxieties, feel more and more relaxed. Relaxed and calm.

Now take a moment to review your body. If you notice any tense places, take a moment increase the tension and then exhale and release the tension. Okay, now you're very relaxed. Now take a moment to inhale and exhale, stretch your body, focus on your surroundings. Get ready to continue the day. Relaxed and calm. Focused and attentive.

Reflections on physical relaxation exercise:

- *How do you feel?*

- *How can you use this activity in your daily life?*

Let the person know that research validates intentional relaxation as a valuable tool for self-care. There are numerous other relaxation exercises you might use as well or you can make up your own and personalize it for a specific person.

2.5 - Other physical exercises for relaxation and stress reduction

(Suggested by Dr. Beverly Ward)

The therapist might have expertise or be able to refer someone to activities such as yoga, adaptive yoga, gentle yoga, tai chi, xigong, and acupuncture. Others find spending time in nature, music, sports, exercise at the gym and similar activities relaxing.

The client can also download free apps. Nike has a number of apps for running and training. There are also free apps for yoga.

Some may find it helpful to create a "Vision Board" to visually remind them of relaxation exercises. Using a poster board or construction paper as a large base, add pictures, drawings, inspiring quotes, etc. as reminders of ways to relax during the day. A relaxation-based Pinterest board may also be useful here.

2.6 - Using self-care and relaxation exercises for closing sessions

You can close sessions by asking the person to summarize what they are taking away from the session and any questions/concerns/goals for the next session(s). You could then end with a short relaxation or self-care exercise.

SECTION THREE: JOURNAL WRITING

3.1 - Exercise: introduce use of journal

(Adapted from Peacebuilding en las Américas Trauma Resiliency workshop and Alternatives to Violence Project.)

Purpose: To help the person reflect on what they are learning, new insights, or reinforce skills.

Instructions: Introduce the idea of writing in a journal. Sometimes it helps to start with "stem" sentences. Ask them to pick a stem and write as much as they would like. They can share with you or keep it just for themselves.

- Although life can be very difficult, we all have things that bring us joy. What gives you joy in your life today?

- What have you learned from the things you've been through in your life?

- When you feel like giving up, what gives you the strength to continue?

- When you feel sad, what do you do to help yourself?

- What personal values have helped you to overcome difficulties?

- How have you overcome everyday stress during the last week?

- Describe some ways you show respect for yourself.

- Describe a personal goal you have for yourself.

- Talk about something you like to do that is fun and also good for you.

Reflections on journal writing

After journal writing during the session or at the next session, reflect with them: What was it like to write in a journal? What did you learn?

3.2 - Exercise: write a dialogue letter in your journal

(Adapted from Peacebuilding en las Américas Trauma Resiliency workshop, and Ira Progoff's At a Journal Workshop. See also the works of Ira Progoff on dialogue journaling.)

Purpose: To use the journal as a way of dialoging about an issue. For example, a dialogue could be with:

- A spiritual being or resource, depending on the person's religious or spiritual background

- A wise person or figure such as a parent or grandparent

Instructions: With this type of journal writing, write as if you are having a conversation about a certain topic. As an example:

- Me: Ever since I got back from Iraq I haven't been able to sleep well. I keep thinking about things over and over.

- Spiritual resource: Well, I think you try not to think about those things during the day and then they pop up at night.

- Me: Yes, I keep hoping if I don't think about them they will go away.

- Spiritual resource: Right, I understand but maybe if we dealt with them during the day you could sleep better at night.

The dialogue could continue from there.

After journal writing during the session, debrief with them. You might ask them to read the dialogue aloud.

Reflections on Dialogue Letter

Ask what it was like to write in a journal. *What did you learn? How do you feel? How can you use this type of journaling in your daily life?*

3.3 - An inspirational journal

- Write down two to three things every day that you are grateful for and try to notice new things/ideas each day. Some people use a regular calendar or an app on a mobile phone.

- Write a reflection to a sacred or inspiring story, quote, prayer, or song, etc.

- Write an insight you had each day.

- Write something you want to share in your next session.

- A visual journal using pictures, drawings, collage, etc.

SECTION FOUR:
ENHANCING PERSONAL / SPIRITUAL / MORAL RESOURCES

Purpose: To explore a person's relationships with others and help identify people/resources who might have been helpful to the veteran in the past and now, and can help the veteran with moral injury.

4.1 - Exercise: Reconnecting with personal, spiritual and moral resources

(With help from Dr. Nina Garcia, LCSW, Ed.D., TEP)

Instructions:

Experience and/or supervision in Gestalt therapy or psychodrama are recommended for the Empty Chair steps 5- 8. An alternate approach would be to use a written dialogue as in the journal exercise.

1. Explain that when people return from war (or have moral injury) they often feel isolated and have trouble reconnecting with resources that can support them and that moral injury often affects our ability to be open to spiritual means of support. You might discuss and write down some ways people either feel abandoned, lost, or disconnected from their spiritual center such as the following, and ask them to add to the list.

   - If God answers all prayers why did XYZ happen?
   - Where was the spirit in all of this?
   - Why do these things happen in the world?

2. Ask the person to talk about who or what has been important to them spiritually and/or any rituals or practices that have been helpful in the past or now - reading sacred texts, prayers, songs, religious/spiritual exercises or practices, etc. Make a list of these together.

3. Give the person a sheet of paper and ask them to think of perhaps 10 people, entities, or forces in their past or now who have had a significant positive influence on them - personally, spiritually, and/or emotionally.

   Perhaps a list might include something like this:

   - God/a spiritual belief

   - A buddy/friend in the service

   - My dad/mom or grandparent

   - My minister when I was in sixth grade

   - Singing

- Walking in the woods

- A favorite teacher or mentor

- My best friend

4. When they are done making the list, ask them pertinent questions like: What helped you feel close to this person, entity, or force? What characteristics did you admire in them and, if you know, what they admired in you? Which people helped you develop your moral and spiritual beliefs?

Would any of these people, entities, or forces be a resource for you now? If you are no longer in contact, is there a way to regain contact? If they are a person who is deceased or inaccessible, what would they probably like to say to you now?

Are there ways you can bring them more into your life now to be a resource for you? Discuss these and write down these ways and help them make a plan on how they might bring the spiritual support more closely into their lives.

5. Empty Chair Steps

- For the purpose of this explanation, the veteran's name is Joe and his resource is his grandfather.

- Ask Joe to pick one of these resources he would like to talk to now. Set up two chairs opposite each other and ask Joe to imagine that his grandfather (his spiritual resource) was across from him and state some of his attributes - what does he look like, what are some of his positive characteristics and strengths that drew you to him, etc.

- Ask the person to change into the chair of the grandfather. Remind him of some of the characteristics "Joe" (for example) said they had and ask him if they agree. "So you are Joe's grandfather. Joe said you are very kind, thoughtful, and loving. Would you be willing to have a conversation with Joe now?" (Most will answer "Yes.")

- Have Joe return to his original seat and ask Joe "What would you like to say to your grandfather today about how he helped you in the past or now?" Or, "Can you remember a specific encounter or event when you felt very close to him that you would like to share with them now?"

- Encourage Joe to go ahead with his statement or question. Then have him change seats and be in the role of the grandfather, to answer the question or make a statement(s). When it seems time, ask Joe to switch back to his chair.

- You will then stand behind the grandfather's chair and remind him what the resource just said.

- You can then encourage Joe to continue with either saying something else he wants to say or ask about.

- Encourage Joe, if he wants to, to ask his grandfather how he could help him and again (even if he has passed away or otherwise not able to communicate) obtain the answer from Joe while he is in the chair of the grandfather.

6. Reflect with the person about what they got from the exercise. What did they think of the process? What would they like to do with what they learned from this exercise? This exercise can also help you as a helper be more in tune with the person's spiritual resource(s).

7. You can also have the person talk to other resources as needed or requested and bring them in as a support at various times during your sessions.

4.2 - Exercise: "River of Life," connecting with one's own resources

(First developed by Cecilia Yocum and Adin Thayer with additional adaptations from Val Liveoak and help from Linda Condon and Christina Bellamy.)

Purpose: To help the participant think about their life and recognize their internal and external resources during their life.

Instructions:

Experience and/or supervision in Gestalt therapy or psychodrama are recommended for steps 8 and 9.

1. Provide an example of a drawing of your own River of Life (with "past," "present," and "future" sections) made in advance on a poster. The drawing could have both positive and negative events in the "past" and "present" sections, and not be too detailed. Also, draw a picture of a future goal, event, or relationship you would like to have in the future. Briefly explain the events depicted.

   Invite the person to draw at least three events in each phase of the River ("past," "present," and "future hoped for event"). Events can be good or not so good, except for those in the "future," which are usually all good.

2. Give the participant paper, markers, crayons, and colored pencils. Have them think about their life like a river, and draw several events along the River. They can add people and places both past and present into the future. (As a variation, the participant can draw a road or trail -- whatever they think best represents their life). They can write words in the picture. (If they do not want to draw or write, invite them to simply sit and think about their past, present and the future.)

3. After the participant finishes the drawing, demonstrate how to process the drawing. The facilitator will set up three chairs representing "past," "present," and "future" (labeled with cards). The facilitator will take notes on a sheet of paper that will later be given to the participant.

4. Ask the person to sit in the chair that says "past" and to show that part of their drawing. Ask them to name the three most important events or relationships in the "past."

5. Ask what were the internal strengths, abilities or skills and external resources that helped them out of the past into the present? These are to be listed on the sheet of paper. It is very important to help them recognize and affirm their internal strengths.

6. Invite the person to sit in the "present" chair and show their drawing, mentioning the three most important events or relationships of the present. Ask about their internal strengths and external resources now. Again, it is very important to help them recognize and affirm their internal strengths.

7. Invite the person to sit in the "future" chair and ask for three important events or relationships they would like to have in the future.

8. Ask if the person wants to experience something of what they envisioned on the paper about their future.

9. Invite the participant to prepare a scene of their future, and have chairs or objects to represent other people or objects. The person takes their own role during this dramatization, and speaks on behalf of the others imagined to be present.

10. After acting out this scene if it is acted out, return to the "future" chair and ask them to name the internal strengths and external resources they have in the future.

11. Invite them to give advice to the "Present-Self" and write about *how to achieve the envisioned future*, as well as what is needed to achieve that "Future-Self." Be sure to ask for specific steps or actions to reach this goal.

12. Then the participant returns to the "present" chair. Invite them to make a promise (commitment) to the "Future Self." They may also speak to the "Past-Self."

13. Write down the commitment and share it with the person.

14. Reflect with the person about what they got from the exercise. What did they think of the process? What would they like to do with what they learned from this exercise?

SECTION FIVE: LISTENING

5.1 - General guidelines

The most important guideline is to help the person feel safe and comfortable and share his or her story with support and no judgment. Practice deep listening: listen from the heart, without comments, relinquish your need of opinions, and respect and embrace his or her truth and story. Allow them to say as much or as little as they would like. It is not necessary for them to tell you any particular details of their stories.

Some people might not want to say anything about incidents related to moral injury and you can let them know that you are willing to hold a space for them in silence, or prayer, or meditation. Do not push anyone to reveal information they do not want to reveal. Let them talk at their own pace, letting them know they have control over how much they wish to say.

5.2 - Writing and then listening

Instructions: Some people will feel better with writing rather than talking. Ask them to write by themselves in a quiet place about an incident where they felt moral injury or conflict. Ask them to write whatever comes to mind without thinking too much about it, and to write freely without attention to grammar or spelling.

Then ask them to come back and share with you what they wrote or just sit with you.

Reflect with the person about what they got from the exercise. What did they think of the process? What would they like to do with what they learned from this exercise? What was it like to talk about the story?

5.3 - Deep listening for facts, feelings and beliefs, values, morals

(Adapted from the Alternatives to Violence Project exercise "Listening in Fours.")

Purpose: To help identify facts, feelings, values, beliefs, and especially moral conflicts. In many instances moral injury occurs when there is a conflict between different values, rather than a lack of values such as "I value and want to save my fellow soldiers and I also do not want to kill other people unnecessarily but I can't do both in this situation." Or, "I would like to stop and help the people by the side of the road because I value them as people but I do not want to endanger my group by stopping to help them."

People might or might not have difficulty recognizing feelings but with moral injury it will also be important to be aware of the facts and especially values and beliefs.

Discuss how combat and war bring forward situations which are unusual for most people and often quick decisions are required involving deep values and beliefs about life. There is usually no time to reflect on them before action is needed. There is a tendency for people to look back later and wonder about their decision and feel remorse.

Instructions: Please note, after the participant tells a story, to be aware of time constraints. That is, allow enough time for the segmenting and processing of the story to allow for natural breaks. It may be necessary to delay some segments to a later session. If this is the case, delay proceeding to additional segments and select exercises to debrief and relax after processing a segment or two. This will allow the telling, processing, and honoring of a segmented story.

1. You could start by giving a short story from your own life to explain the process if you have a situation that is not too detailed. After you have told the story ask the person to help you complete a grid:

   - Make three columns.

   - In the first column list important facts from the story.

   - In the second column brainstorm and list the feelings from the story.

   - In the third column write a list of conflicts between values and beliefs which that situation might generate. Often there are clashing values or morals rather than a lack of morals.

   - Reflect on how these feelings and values could conflict.

2. Next, discuss the types of issues that soldiers with moral injury encounter. Brainstorm about the kinds of situations someone with moral injury issues might have encountered in the service. Use the list of situations from some of the readings/videos from the list of resources in Section 10 if needed or from their own experience. Pick one situation and make three columns.

   - In the first column write down possible facts that might occur in that scenario.

   - Brainstorm the kinds of feelings that might come up in that scenario in a column next to it.

   - In the third column write a list of possible values and beliefs which that situation might generate. Again, there are often clashing values/morals rather than a lack of morals.

   - Reflect on these feelings and values or beliefs.

3. Ask the person if they would like you to help identify the feelings and values in one of their stories. If not, ask if they want to try another one from the moral injury resources. If they have a personal story they are willing to share, ask them to tell their story in short segments so there is time to look at each segment if needed. You might have them tell the whole story first and then decide how they would like to break them into segments, if needed. Allow time for processing each segment, since each part is important. You might need to spend time to allow for feelings to be fully expressed.

   - As they finish talking about each segment, make a similar grid as above.

- In the first column write down the facts that occurred in that segment.

- Write down the feelings they had in that segment of the story in the second column next to it and talk about them.

- In the third column write a list of values and beliefs which that situation generated. Again, there are often clashing values/morals rather than a lack of morals.

- Reflect on these feelings and values or beliefs and discuss as needed.

4. Reflect on these feelings and values/beliefs with the person. Were there any new facts, feelings, values, or beliefs they noticed? Did they see any clashes that they were unaware of at the time?

5. At this point ask if the person would like to take time for an activity such as:

- Journal writing

- Empty chair work with a spiritual resource

- Spending some time in prayer or meditation or inspirational reading

6. At the end, ask the person to reflect how they are feeling. Reflect on the exercise with questions and comments, such as:

- What did you learn?

- Did you make any surprising discoveries?

- Would you like to look at any other incidents at another session?

- What was it like to talk with me about the story?

5.4 - Listening for responsibility and guilt - a different way of looking at a problem

Purpose: To help someone see that a problem might have many different causes, and that seen and unseen forces may have affected the situation.

People often take on too much responsibility or none. Working to understand the right amount can help them perceive the reality of the situation and help them take appropriate action.

They can also sometimes confuse feeling guilty with being responsible and it might be helpful to sort those feelings out as well.

Instructions:

1. Think of an example from your own life where you felt moral injury for the sake of explaining the process. For this example, I give a situation where I tried to catch a stray dog but he ran into traffic and was killed.

2. Give an example of rating the event:

    *   Standing on a line with imaginary numbers, I would then rate myself from 0 to 100 on how guilty I felt. At first I put myself at 100.

    *   Next standing on a line with imaginary numbers, I would then rate myself from 0 to 100 on how much responsibility I felt. At first I put myself at 100.

    *   Looking at the situation I felt really bad and felt the accident was totally my fault. I should not have tried to catch him and he might have just run down a side street.

3. Next think if there were there any other people responsible? An unseen person was the driver of the car that hit him. Were there any others? Then I considered that the dog's owner had some responsibility.

    *   I then rated the owner as 45% and the driver at 10% along an imaginary bar graph.

    *   Then I would rate again how guilty I felt on the line. I now felt about 80%.

    *   Even with 45% responsibility in this situation, was there anything I could have done differently?

    *   What could others have done differently?

    *   If I wanted to make amends what could I do?

    In this example, a possible response might be:

    "I decided to do research on what to do if you see a dog running and learned that I should have run away from the dog and tried to get him to run after me. I also decided I wanted to make amends to myself and forgive myself for possibly making the wrong choice."

4. Get an example from the veteran if they are willing to try this:

"What is a problem you have been thinking about that is bothering you? Please explain the event." Ask them to first identify the different people or forces involved (both seen and unseen). Be sure to include forces such as certain rules, certain routines, etc. Go slow with this since people frequently want to rush through. Helping them go slowly will help them understand what was happening around them which they were not able to process at the time.

Ask the veteran to rate the event:

- Standing on a line with imaginary numbers, ask them to rate themselves from 0 to 100 on how *guilty* they felt or feel.

- Next, standing on a line with imaginary numbers, ask them to rate themselves from 0 to 100 on how much *responsibility* they felt or feel.

- Next, think about the other people/entities responsible (seen or unseen)?

- Then ask them to give a percentage of how much <u>*responsibility and guilt*</u> each *other* person, force, or entity had along the imaginary line. Don't try to absolve them of any responsibility since that is not helpful unless it was a situation where they were truly helpless.

5. Ask the veteran to reflect on their own responsibility and either discuss or journal on the topics:

- "I am responsible for _____"

- "I am not responsible for _____"

- Use as many of these types of sentences as needed. Discuss the responses with the person.

6. Ask the veteran what they would like to do with these observations such as: "Forgive yourself? Forgive someone else? Make amends? Take some positive action?" Let them know that there will be an opportunity for them to talk with a Forgiving Spirit if they would like. (See Section Six on Forgiveness.)

7. Reflecting on their actions or lack of action, ask them: "Were the actions due to a lack of skill, a lack of education, a moral fault, or something else? What might you have done differently if you had had more knowledge, more skill, more time, more support, or a different circumstance, etc.?"

- Ask the veteran to "take some time to go back and imagine yourself and notice those moments when something could have been different. Say a prayer or have a moment of silence (or some way of sending compassion/forgiveness) for yourself and others at that time. Practice as many times as you would like."

- Ask the veteran to imagine practicing this method in their daily life.

- Explain that rather than using these moments to "beat themselves up," which people often do when they feel they have made a mistake, "use this time as a way of forgiveness with prayer, meditation or some positive activity."

- Suggest that they start a "Self-Compassion Journal" where they write kind things to themselves as if they were one of their personal and spiritual resources.

8. Reflect on the responsibility of others. Was the responsibility due to a lack of skill, a lack of education, a moral fault, or something else?

9. Is there anything they would want to do to help correct these problems? For example, one soldier developed some new procedures for handling similar situations. Make a list of possible options, research to be done, etc., if appropriate.

SECTION SIX: FORGIVENESS

6.1 - What does forgiveness mean to you?

(Some questions adapted from Alternatives to Violence Project)

Purpose: To discover what forgiveness means to the person.

Instructions:

1. Ask the person to reflect on these questions either with you or in a journal:

   - What does forgiveness mean to you?

   - Do you believe that forgiveness is possible?

     If not, ask what is the message that keeps them from believing they cannot be forgiven? (This might require doing some deeper work about messages they got when they were younger or in other circumstance. You could consider using cognitive therapy to deal with irrational beliefs or methods that you have worked with before in counseling.)

   - Think of a time you were forgiven and what that felt like?

   - Think of a time you forgave someone else and what that felt like?

   - Think of a time you would like to be forgiven.

   - If you woke up tomorrow and were forgiven, imagine how that would feel?

   - Think of a time you would like to forgive someone.

   - If you woke up tomorrow and forgave them, imagine how that would feel?

2. Reflect with the person about what they got from the exercise. What did they think of the process? What would they like to do with what they learned from this exercise? Did they see any conflicting answers? Which responses could help you the most?

3. Is there someone from their religious/spiritual tradition that they would like to talk to in person? Discuss how they might arrange time with to talk to them.

6.2 – Exercise: Initial conversation with the Forgiving Spirit

(with help from Dr. Nina Garcia, LCSW, Ed.D., TEP)

Purpose: To talk with a spirit with whom they can speak openly and share about their feelings and seek forgiveness or forgive someone else, to have a witness for forgiveness, and to help the person see that they have the answers within themselves.

For some people a Forgiving Spirit might be a religious figure such as God, Jesus, or a particular saint. Others might have a spiritual resource such as a wise and supportive person from their past, a favorite fictional character, etc. The important point is that this figure should be supportive and forgiving.

(Experience and or supervision in Gestalt therapy or psychodrama are recommended for this exercise, and exercises 6.3 and 6.4 below. An adaptation would be asking the person to imagine a conversation with the Forgiving Spirit or writing a dialogue on paper and then talking with you about the experience.)

Instructions:

(For the purpose of this explanation, the veteran's name is John.)

1. Ask John to talk about his reflections on forgiveness.

2. Ask John if there is a specific incident he would like to discuss. If he has not already worked through the exercises "Listening for facts and feelings, and beliefs, values and morals," and "Listening for responsibility and guilt," ask him to go through these first with you, since that will help you as the facilitator guide him with this exercise.

3. Tell John that for the purposes of the exercise, he will dialogue with a "Forgiving Spirit" that he will picture or imagine and talk with.

4. Ask John "What are the main attributes of your Forgiving Spirit?" If John states negative traits, remind him that the Forgiving Spirit is a positive force.

5. Set up two chairs opposite each other and ask John to imagine that the Forgiving Spirit is across from him. Ask him to state some of their attributes.

6. Ask John to change into the chair of the Forgiving Spirit. Remind him of some of the characteristics John said they had as the Forgiving Spirit and ask him if they agree. Ask him to say something about some of their attributes.

7. Have John return to his original seat and ask him "What would you like to talk with the Forgiving Spirit about today? Would you like help forgiving yourself or forgiving someone else?"

    For example:

    John might ask say to the Forgiving Spirit: "I still feel horrible and guilty about the time when I saw the child with what I thought was a suicide vest and shot him without knowing if he was actually wearing a suicide vest."

If he says he would like help forgiving himself, proceed to section 6.3. If he wants to forgive someone else proceed to 6.4. During different sessions, a person might choose between section 6.3 and 6.4.

6.3 – Exercise: Talking with the Forgiving Spirit about forgiveness for oneself

(Continued from Section 6.2 above)

1. Have John return to his original seat and ask him, "What help would you like from your Forgiving Spirit today?

For example:

In the seat of the Forgiving Spirit, John (as the Forgiving Spirit) might say something like, "John, I know you were not sure what to do in that situation and you had only a few seconds to decide before you and your buddies might have been blown up. That must have been really terrible for you. What were you feeling?"

2. Switch John back into his chair and allow him to respond. Ask John what questions he has for the Forgiving Spirit. Perhaps John says he would like to ask how to deal with some of the guilt he is feeling.

3. Switch back to the Forgiving Spirit and ask John as the Forgiving Spirit to respond.

4. If John is stuck, you as the counselor, might say something like:

"I am going to suggest some things you could say to John as the Forgiving Spirit and see if any of these feel right for you as the Forgiving Spirit." Then make some possible suggestions and let him try out ones he thinks would fit for him. Then ask John to return to his seat.

5. You will then stand behind (but not sit in) the Forgiving Spirit's chair, and remind John what the Forgiving Spirit just said.

   - You can then encourage John to continue with either saying something else he wants to say or ask about.

   - Encourage John, if he wants to, to ask the Forgiving Spirit how the Forgiving Spirit could help him and again obtain the answer from the Forgiving Spirit while John is in the chair of the Forgiving Spirit.

For example:

   - John as himself might say something like, "What can I do when I start to feel bad about killing that child?"

   - John, as the Forgiving Spirit, might tell him something like, "When you feel that way, remember that I am here by you."

6. End with John back in his own seat and saying the last thing he would like to say to the Forgiving Spirit.

7. Debrief with John about what he got from the exercise. Allow some time for prayer, breathing, or silence to allow John to process the experience. Ask if he has any remaining questions or concerns before moving on or ending the session.

8. This exercise can be repeated at another session with the same or different incidents. Take whatever time is needed to work through these incidents.

6.4 - Exercise: Talking with the Forgiving Spirit about forgiving someone else

(For the purpose of this explanation, the veteran's name is John.)

1. Set up three chairs. One for the person/entity they would like to forgive and across from that chair, two chairs: one for John and one for the Forgiving Spirit. John will rotate between those two chairs but will ***not*** take the chair of the person/entity he wants to forgive.

2. Explain to John that forgiveness is a process and that the process will probably take a while. He might have to work on this over a number of sessions and take breaks as needed.

3. John might say to the Forgiving Spirit: "I would like to forgive the person who put that suicide vest on that child because _____ "

Allow John to say as much as he wants. Expect that John might cry or be very angry.

4. Then have John change seats and be in the role of the Forgiving Spirit to answer a question or make a statement(s).

For example:

In the seat of the Forgiving Spirit, John (as the Forgiving Spirit) might say something like "John, I know you are very angry/upset about what happened. That must have been really terrible for you. It is important that you start by telling them what they did wrong and how it affected you (and other people or events). Please tell _____ (pointing to the chair across from them) what they did wrong and what the consequences were.

5. Switch John back into his chair and allow him to respond and talk to the person in the third chair and say what he wants to say. Allow as much time as needed.

6. Switch John back to the Forgiving Spirit chair, and then ask him if there is anything else he wants to say to the "other person."

7. If the person is stuck, you as the counselor might say something like:

"I am going to suggest some things you could say to John as the Forgiving Spirit. See if any of these feel right for you as the Forgiving Spirit." Make some suggestions and let him try out ones he thinks would fit for him. Then ask John to return to his seat.

8. You will stand behind (rather than in) the Forgiving Spirit's chair and remind John what the Forgiving Spirit just said.

9. You can then encourage John to continue saying anything else they want to say.

10. Encourage John, if he wants to, to ask the Forgiving Spirit how the Forgiving Spirit could help him with forgiveness and again obtain the answer from the Forgiving Spirit, while John is in the chair of the Forgiving Spirit.

11. End with John back in his own seat and say the last thing he would like to say to "the other person," and then to the Forgiving Spirit.

12. Debrief with John about what he got from the exercise. Allow some time for prayer, breathing, or silence to allow him to process the experience. Ask if he has any remaining questions or concerns before moving on or ending the session.

This exercise can be repeated at another session with the same or different incidents. Take whatever time the client needs to work through these incidents.

6.5 - Exercise: Letter asking for forgiveness

Experience and/or supervision in Gestalt therapy or psychodrama are recommended for step 5. Or, the client could read the letter to an empty chair and not change seats.

(For the purpose of this explanation, the veteran's name is John.)

Instructions:

1. Ask John if he wants to write a letter asking for forgiveness. This is not a letter he will necessarily send to someone.

2. Assuming that John does want to write a letter, ask him to go to a desk in the room and write the letter. Suggest that he include what he thinks he did wrong, acknowledge his role, state how he feels about his role and what he might be able to do make the situation better, or make amends.

3. Ask John to read the letter out loud if he would like to, either to you or the Forgiving Spirit (or both).

4. If John only wants to read it to you, just sit in your seat and listen. Then ask him to reflect on what it was like to write the letter and hear it read out loud. Ask if he want any feedback from you.

5. If John wants to read it to the Forgiving Spirit, try these steps:

    (a) Set up two chairs opposite each other and ask John to imagine that the Forgiving Spirit is across from him. Ask John to state again some of the attributes of the Forgiving Spirit.

    (b) Ask John to change into the chair of the Forgiving Spirit. Remind him of some of the characteristics John said the Forgiving Spirit has, and ask him, as the Forgiving Spirit, if he does have these attributes.

    (c) Have John move back to his seat, and read the letter to the Forgiving Spirit.

    (d) Next, John should go back in the seat of the Forgiving Spirit. Read John's letter to the Forgiving Spirit while standing behind John's chair.

    (e) Allow John as the Forgiving Spirit to make a response. If he is stuck, you the counselor might say something like: "I am going to suggest some things you could say to John as the Forgiving Spirit. See if any of these feel right for you as the Forgiving Spirit." Then make some suggestions and let him try out ones he thinks would fit for him.

    (f) Then return John to his chair and say the last thing he would like to say to the Forgiving Spirit at this time.

    (g) Ask him to reflect on what it was like to write the letter and hear it read out loud. Ask if he wants any feedback from you.

6.6 - Letter giving forgiveness

Experience and/or supervision in Gestalt therapy or psychodrama are recommended for step 3 if you use the empty chair method.

(For the purpose of this explanation, the veteran's name is John.)

Instructions:

1. There might be situations where the veteran would like to forgive someone who they are not able to communicate with or is no longer available due to death or other factors. Writing the letter is a way of expressing what they would like to say but perhaps cannot say. This is not a letter they will necessarily send to someone.

2. Assuming that they want to do this, ask them to go to a desk in the room and write the letter. Suggest that they include what they think they did wrong, acknowledge their role,

state how they are feeling about their role and what they might be able to do to make the situation better or make amends.

3. Ask them to read the letter out loud if they would like either to you or the Forgiving Spirit (preferred method), using the empty chair method above.

4. Reflect on what it was like to write the letter and hear the letter out loud.

SECTION SEVEN: MAKING AMENDS

Purpose: Making amends means to put something right or change or modify it for the better. People often feel inept at first when thinking about making amends.

7.1 - Discovering resources to make amends

Instructions: Explain that making amends is another way people deal with moral injury situations. Review with the person some of the ideas from the River of Life exercise, their internal and external resources, and their goals for themselves.

1. Make a list of important roles they have had in the armed forces or outside the armed forces, in the community and at home. Ask them to pick out the top ten most satisfying for them.

2. Write down what impact they made on others and themselves in these roles.

3. Do they see any transfer of the skills they had from these roles that they could use in making amends? Make a list of these.

7.2 - Exercise: Discovering what amends to make

Experience and/or supervision in Gestalt therapy or psychodrama are recommended for steps 5-7.

Instructions:

1. Go back to the exercise on guilt and responsibility. Ask them to restate which ones they now feel they had responsibility for in some way.

2. Discuss whether it is possible or beneficial to make direct amends or indirect amends. For example, they might make indirect amends to someone who is a refugee or someone who is injured in the U.S. Finding situations that are somewhat similar in nature might be a good fit for making amends.

3. However, not all issues related to moral injury will have a good fit but it might be possible to find a related issue.

4. Ask the person to pick amends they would like to make and describe what a scene from what that would look like.

5. Invite them to prepare a scene of making amends using chairs, furniture and objects to represent other people or objects. Ask the person to take their own role during this dramatization. If they are reluctant to step into a scene, ask them to imagine the scene.

6. Have them step into (or imagine themselves stepping into) the scene and feel like what it would be like to be making amends.

7. Ask them to step out of the scene and comment about how they feel about this type of making amends. Reflect on what they liked or didn't like.

8. Repeat with as many types of amends making situations as needed.

9. Reflect with the person which of these above amends making they would like to try.

If the person is unable to come up with any ideas, you might look at these alternatives:

- Suggest that they do some research either online or in their community about projects they might possibly participate in. One interesting program is the Heroic Imagination Project, which provides training on how to take effective action in challenging situations. Research has found that people are rarely aware or trained about how to take action quickly. The project uses volunteers to take the learning from research out into the world and help people respond more effectively.

- Some people might be looking for ways to change certain military procedures to reduce the negative effects of war, especially to civilians. Some soldiers have been effective in writing and submitting new procedures.

- Some might see a different job they would like within the service.

- Some people might want to reexamine being involved in war or being in the service. Programs like Quaker House (www.quakerhouse.org) might be able to help with that discernment or perhaps there are similar resources in their community.

- Some people might be interested in a VA-sponsored or independent veterans' support groups, service projects, or other local resources.

7.3 - Exercise: Making amends

Instructions:

1. If the person can come up with a way to make amends that they would like to try, ask them to describe it to you and talk about the steps involved in the way they would like to make amends.

2. Depending on their decision, they might like to discuss with you how the steps in making amends are going.

3. Reflect with them what it was like to take those steps and discuss the next steps. How are they feeling?

4. Discuss with them that even after making amends there might still be a feeling of moral injury. What are personal, spiritual, and social resources that could support them? You could then do another round of empty chair work.

SECTION EIGHT: HEALING RITUALS

(Adapted from Peacebuilding en las Américas Trauma Resiliency workshop, and help from Linda Condon and Christina Bellamy)

8.1 - Exercise: A positive significant/meaningful moment

Purpose: To have a way to honor grief and loss.

Instructions: A ritual is a way of honoring a process of grief and loss. Many times they have not had the times or circumstances or ability to honor their loss. This ritual will allow someone to honor their losses through remembering a significant or meaningful moment connected with the person or place or thing.

1. Ask the person to draw "a positive significant or meaningful moment" connected with the person or place or thing they have lost.

2. Ask them to imagine that significant or meaningful moment happening again, or imagine a conversation with that person.

3. Ask the person to talk about and describe what the positive significant or meaningful moment was. What were some characteristics of the person or the scene of the event? Describe the person or scene in as much detail as they would like, including other significant people in the scene.

4. Next ask them to light a candle to remember the moment or person. They will light their candle from a large candle that symbolizes healing.

5. Ask them if they would like to say anything else.

6. Allow for time for silence or a song or prayer.

8.2 - Exercise: Creating a ritual with the person's beliefs

Purpose: To develop a ritual that seems right for the person's personal and spiritual beliefs.

Instructions:

1. Ask the person if there are any rituals within their spiritual or religious beliefs that could help them heal.

2. If there are, help them design the ritual according to their beliefs.

3. Help them, if they wish, set up the ritual. Find out if they want to invite other people such as some of their personal supporters.

4. If they would prefer performing the ritual just with you, ask them if they want to set up a chair for any of the personal or spiritual resources from some of the first exercises to be "participating."

5. Ask then to think of any music, prayers, or activities they would like for the ritual.

6. Perform the ritual and then reflect on the experience.

SECTION NINE: CLOSING

You should use your usual closing sessions you use with other clients including the following, which might also be discussed during the entire counseling process:

- An evaluation of the overall process

- What was helpful or not helpful?

- Was something left unfinished?

- Does the client have goals that you or someone else could help them with?

- Are there other resources they need?

- Appreciations of their work

- Does the client want to set up a schedule for additional or follow-up sessions?

SECTION 10: BIBLIOGRAPHY AND RESOURCES

Compiled by Quaker House, 223 Hillside Ave, Fayetteville, NC 28301, 910-323-3912, qpr@quaker.org

Afterwar: Healing the Moral Wounds of our Soldiers
by Nancy Sherman

At a Journal Workshop – The basic text and guide for using the intensive journal
Ira Progoff
Dialogue House Library, 1975

Bridging Chaplaincy and Mental Health
A DVD Video series sponsored by the Department Of Defense and the Department of Veterans Affairs.

Coming Home: Ministry That Matters with Veterans and Military Families
by Zachary Moon

Moral Injury: New Interventions, Theological Reflection
Rev. Peter E. Bauer, LCSW, LMFT, LCDC, ACSW, BCD

Moral Injury
by Alice Lynd with the assistance of Staughton Lynd, 2015, Quaker House

Peace at Last: Stories of Hope and Healing for Veterans and Their Families
by Deborah L. Grassman

PTSD: The Sacred Wound, HEALTH PROGRESS by Edward Tick, Ph.D.
The Military Chaplain, Fall 2014

Soul Repair: Recovering from Moral Injury after War by Rev. Rita Nakashima Brock and Gabriella Lettini *http://brite.edu/academics/programs/soul-repair/*
The Grunts: Damned if They Kill, Damned if They Don't by David Wood for Huffington Post:
http://projects.huffingtonpost.com/moral-injury/the-grunts

The Impact of Killing on Mental Health Symptoms and Functioning in War Veterans
Shira Maguen, Ph.D. March 23, 2011 San Francisco VA Medical Center

Trauma, Loss and Moral Injury: Different Approached for Prevention and Treatment
Nash, W. P., Westphal, R.J., and Litz, B. Armed Forces Public Health Conference (3/23/11)

Moral Injury

A Presentation of Quaker House Military Counseling Center

Origin of Concept of Moral Injury

Dr. Jonathan Shay is a doctor and clinical psychiatrist. While working at the United State Department of Veteran's Affairs outpatient clinic in Boston, Shay was struck by the similarity of the story of Achilles told in Homer's "Illiad" and the stories he was hearing from veterans. He coined the term "moral injury."

Dr. Brett Litz, a clinical psychologist with the VA Boston Healthcare system, defined moral injury in 2009 as "perpetrating, failing to prevent, bearing witness to, or learning about acts that transgress deeply held moral beliefs and expectations."

Moral Injury Definitions:

- "A deep sense of transgression including feelings of shame, grief, meaninglessness, and remorse from having violated core moral beliefs." Rev. Rita *Nakashima Brock and Gabriella Lettini, Soul Repair*

- "A violation of conscience regarding what a person did, or sometimes what the person did not do, in a morally ambiguous situation under authority in a military system." *CDR David Thompson, CHC, USNR (Ret) The Military Chaplain*

Moral Injury is not officially recognized by the Defense Department and is not accepted as a psychiatric diagnosis. But it is moral injury, not PTSD, that is increasingly acknowledged as the signature wound of this generation of veterans: a bruise on the soul, akin to grief or sorrow, with lasting impact on the individuals and their families.

MULTIPLE DEPLOYMENTS FOR TROOPS IN RECENT WARS

Frequent deployments to Afghanistan and Iraq have become routine for American soldiers – raising the risk of lasting mental trauma.

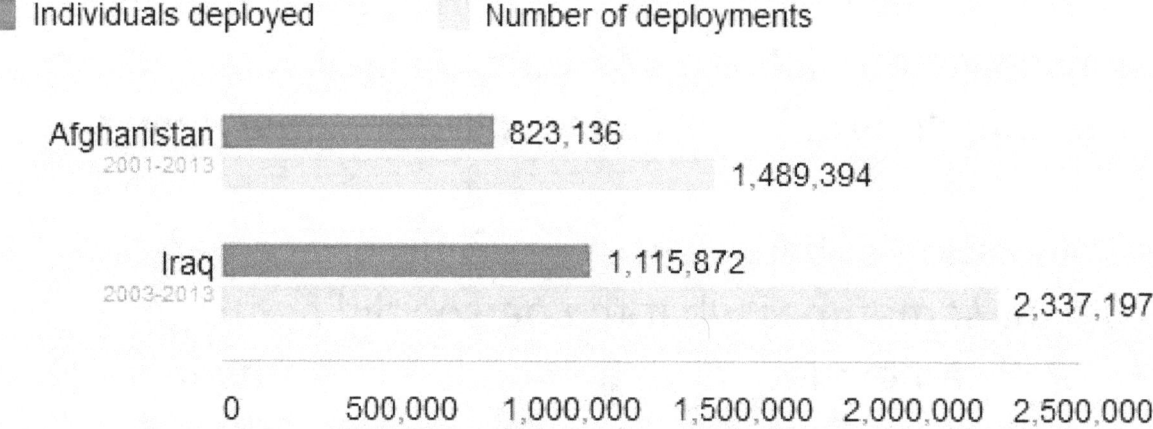

▮ Individuals deployed   ▯ Number of deployments

Afghanistan
2001-2013
823,136
1,489,394

Iraq
2003-2013
1,115,872
2,337,197

0   500,000   1,000,000   1,500,000   2,000,000   2,500,000

Source: U.S. Department of Defense

PTSD

- The physical response to fear and danger, hyper-alertness and rise in adrenaline, necessary for survival in combat becomes an involuntary reaction to a remembered life threatening fear

- Triggered by crowds, noise, an argument

- Can be quickly diagnosed and therapy available

Moral Injury

Not fear but exposure - an experience or set of experiences that can provoke mild or intense grief, shame, or guilt

War trauma symptoms: The symptoms of PTSD and Moral Injury and how they overlap

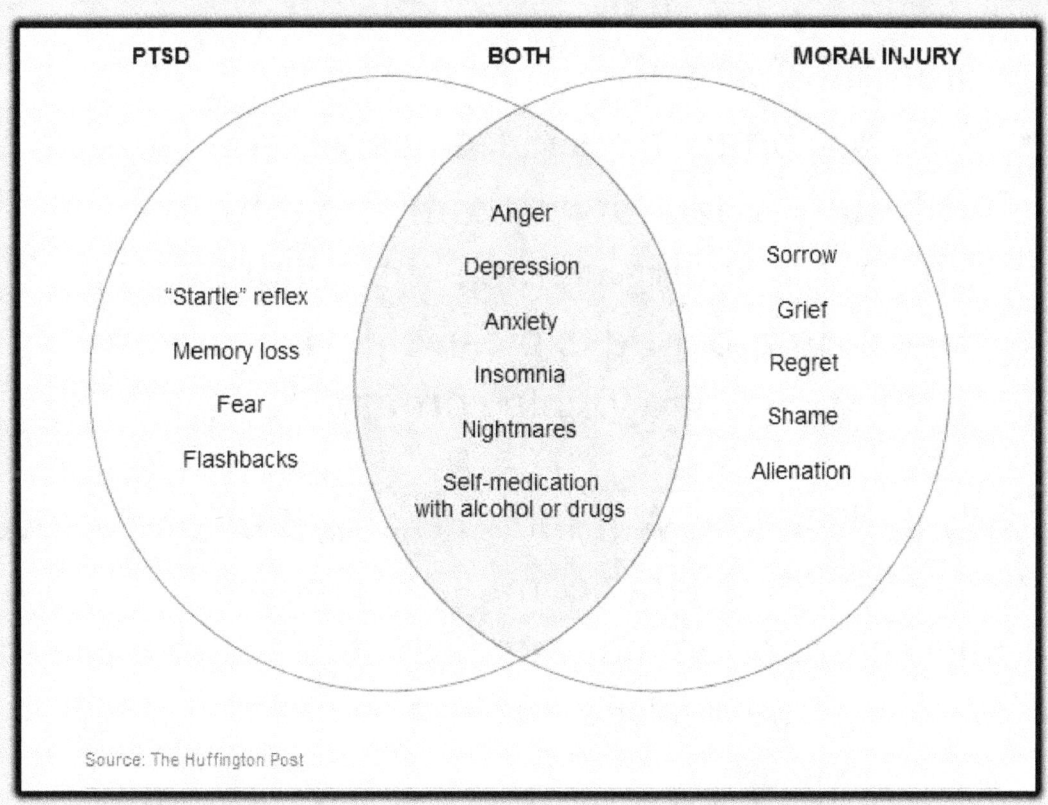

PTSD | BOTH | MORAL INJURY

PTSD
- "Startle" reflex
- Memory loss
- Fear
- Flashbacks

BOTH
- Anger
- Depression
- Anxiety
- Insomnia
- Nightmares
- Self-medication with alcohol or drugs

MORAL INJURY
- Sorrow
- Grief
- Regret
- Shame
- Alienation

Source: The Huffington Post

TROOPS SEE THINGS THEY CAN'T FORGET

A study of 3,761 paratroopers and Marines after their return from combat in Iraq in late 2003 found grim results about troops' exposure to morally damaging events.

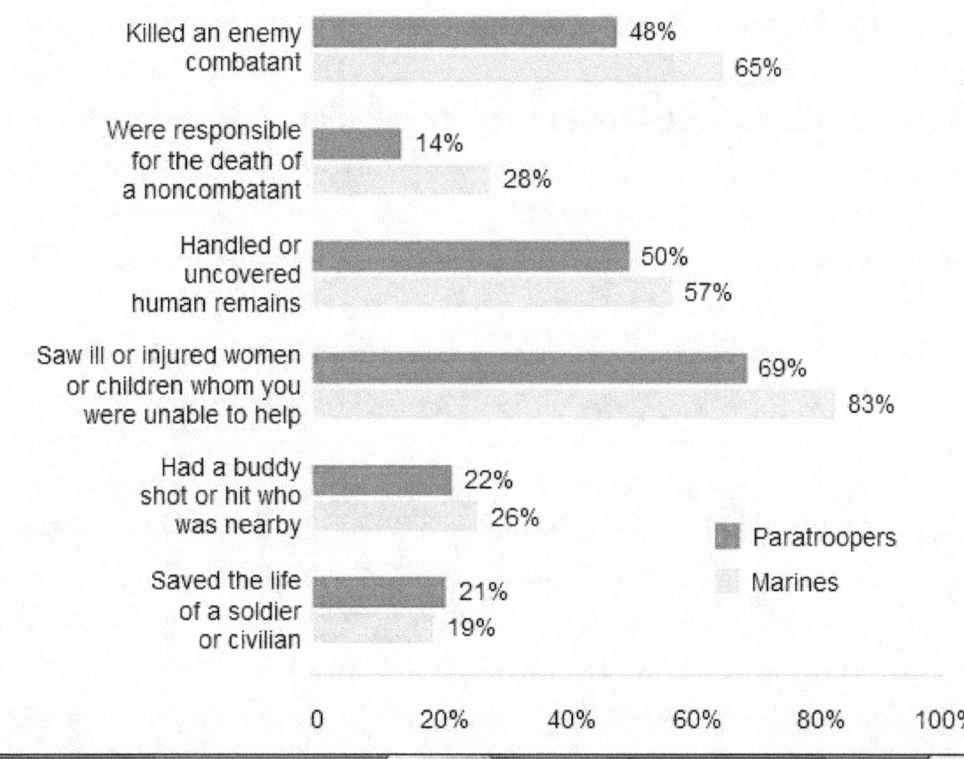

Killed an enemy combatant — 48% / 65%

Were responsible for the death of a noncombatant — 14% / 28%

Handled or uncovered human remains — 50% / 57%

Saw ill or injured women or children whom you were unable to help — 69% / 83%

Had a buddy shot or hit who was nearby — 22% / 26%

Saved the life of a soldier or civilian — 21% / 19%

■ Paratroopers
■ Marines

0   20%   40%   60%   80%   100%

Factors worsening Moral Injury:

- Iraq and Afghanistan wars lack moral clarity
- Combat often takes place in civilian setting
- Difficulty in identifying combatant from civilian, including women and children
- Use of improvised explosive device kills and wounds with no visible combatant

A study early in Iraq War found that 2/3rds of deployed Marines killed an enemy combatant, more than half had handled human remains, and 28% felt responsible for the death of an Iraqi civilian

THE WOUNDS THAT DON'T SHOW

Mental health wounds far outnumbered physical injuries in Iraq and Afghanistan.

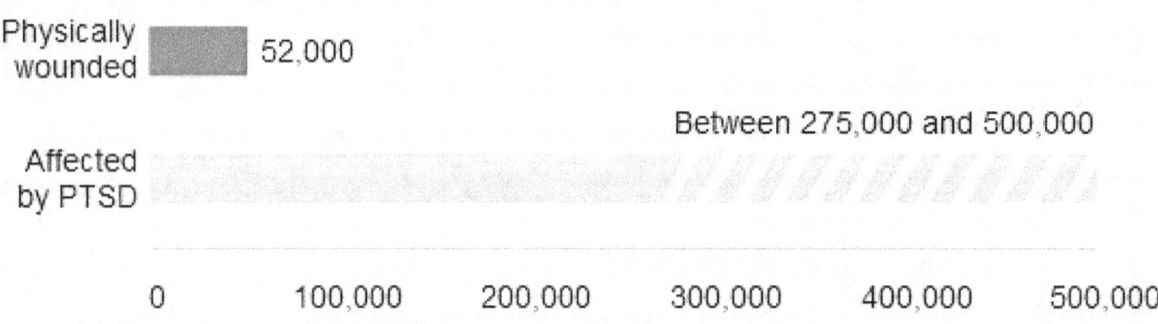

Physically wounded — 52,000

Between 275,000 and 500,000

Affected by PTSD

| 0 | 100,000 | 200,000 | 300,000 | 400,000 | 500,000 |

Source: U.S. Department of Defense, U.S. Department of Veterans Affairs

What is the military doing about it?

- "Resiliency" training before deployments: training in physical and psychological strengthening

- Embedding mental health care professionals into combat battalions

- Leaders are being trained to recognize soldiers under severe stress and get them help

- The Pentagon has funded a $2 million clinical trial to explore adapting PTSD therapies for moral injury

- Defense Department and Veterans Administration have nothing specifically for Moral Injury, saying it's "not defined" and that there is no "formal diagnosis" for it. However, they "provide a wide range of medical and non-medical resources.... in addressing it."

Learning to Live with Moral Injury
What Helps?

- Treatments for PTSD do not work for Moral Injury (re-living event, medication, etc.)

- Focus on helping soldier accept that wrong was done, but that it need not define his/her life

- Rituals of cleansing and forgiveness

- Help soldier feel safe and comfortable and share his/her story with support and no judgment. Practice deep listening: listen from heart, without comments, relinquish your need of opinions, respect and embrace his/her truth and story

What Helps? (Continued)

- Support for healthy lifestyle

- Have safe space for seating

- Learn to be with anger and grief

- Ask: "What can we do to support you?"

- Write imaginary letter of apology to those involved

- Encourage involvement in the arts: writing, music, art, dance

- Imaginary conversation with a compassionate moral authority

What Helps? (Continued)

- **Work to understand the division of responsibility:**

Example: Soldier kills child who has a grenade

- 50%: the terrorist who told the child to throw the grenade

- 20%: what soldier did

- 20%: the squad leader who ordered the shoot

- 10%: what child did

What Helps? (Continued)

- The veteran stands in a group of fellow veterans and says, "This is what happened. This is what I saw. This is what I did," and their fellow veterans nod and say, "I hear you. I hear you." And just accept it, without saying, "Well, you couldn't help it," or, "You're really a good person at heart."

- **Offer ways to make amends and create a new life purpose: disaster relief, peace missions, service projects, community service, acts of kindness, working with animals, farming**

Atonement and Penance:

Suggestions from Brian Meyer, Ph.D., LCP, Interim Associate Chief, Mental Health/Supervisory Psychologist, H. H. McGuire VA Medical Center, Richmond, VA

When positive action fails:

- **Atonement:** what actions would it take to "balance the scale"?

- **Penance:** actions that will bring pain and/or suffering, such as giving a great deal of money to a charity or humanitarian work that is difficult

New interventions for moral injury are currently being tested:

Impact Of Killing In War (IOK) and
Adaptive Disclosure (AD)

Both interventions are being developed through the Department Of Veterans Affairs and the Defense Center For Psychological Health.

Impact Of Killing in War
A six-session module

Includes:
Education about the complex interplay of bio-psychosocial aspects of killing in war that may cause inner conflict and moral injury.

Adaptive Disclosure (AD)

An eight-session intervention that takes into account the unique aspects of the phenomenology of military service in war in order to address difficulties such as moral injury and traumatic loss that are not explicitly addressed in current treatment interventions for PTSD.

"These sessions provide tools for the journey of healing."

Brian Meyer, Ph.D., LCP, Supervisory Psychologist, H. H. McGuire VA

Acceptance and Commitment Therapy (ACT)

• Accept what is out of one's personal control, and commit to action that improves and enriches life.

• Teaches psychological skills to deal with painful thoughts and feelings effectively - in such a way that they have much less impact and influence. (Mindfulness)

• Helps to clarify what is truly important and meaningful - i.e values - then uses that knowledge to guide, inspire and motivate to change one's life for the better.

Moral Injury:
New Interventions, Theological Reflection
Rev. Peter E. Bauer
LCSW, LMFT, LCDC, ACSW, BCD

Healing from Moral Injury is a Life-Long Process

- It doesn't happen over night; it doesn't happen all at once.

- This is hard work to do not only for the patient, service member, family member but also for the Chaplain, Mental Health provider.

- Encourage patients, service members, family members, and providers to take the work slow.

- Take pauses, breaks, breathe, reflect to see how the work is going.

- Consult with others when necessary.

- Pray, meditate for whom you are working with and for yourself.

- Know that we all deserve to experience healing in our lives.

- We all need to be able to walk in to the light out of darkness.

- May it be so for us all.

"Through our work on moral injury, we work to foster communities which can understand that war and its aftermath belong to all of us and are our responsibility."

Rev. Rita Nakashima Brock

"Our veterans have been on the deepest and darkest of journeys 'through the valley of the shadow.' It is our collective responsibility to hear their soul cries of distress, respond with all they need, and take the moral and spiritual journeys home with them. Healing our veterans heals, teaches, transforms and blesses us all."

Edward Tick, Ph.D.

Government Help

For help with moral injury or other mental health issues

The Defense Centers of Excellence for Psychological Health and Traumatic Brain Injury's 24/7 live chat outreach center (also at 866-966-1020 or email resources@dcoeoutreach.org).

The Pentagon website Military OneSource for short-term, non-medical counseling.

Veterans can call, text or chat with the Veterans Crisis Line. Dial 800-273-8255.

References:

The Grunts: Damned if They Kill, Damned if They Don't
by David Wood for Huffington Post:
http://projects.huffingtonpost.com/moral-injury/the-grunts

Soul Repair: Recovering from Moral Injury after War
By Rev. Rita Nakashima Brock and Gabriella Lettini
http://brite.edu/academics/programs/soul-repair/

PTSD: The Sacred Wound, HEALTH PROGRESS
By Edward Hicks, Ph.D.

The Military Chaplain, Fall 2014

"Bridging Chaplaincy And Mental Health:"
A DVD Video series sponsored by the Department Of Defense and the Department Of Veterans Affairs.

The Impact of Killing on Mental Health Symptoms and Functioning in War Veterans, Shira Maguen, Ph.D. March 23, 2011 San Francisco VA Medical Center

Moral Injury: New Interventions, Theological Reflection,
Rev. Peter E. Bauer, LCSW, LMFT, LCDC, ACSW, BCD

www.actmindfully.com

www.ingramcontent.com/pod-product-compliance
Lightning Source LLC
Chambersburg PA
CBHW081118280526
45787CB00007B/2892